John E. Winkler

A Cherished Wilderness

The Adirondacks

A Cherished Wilderness
The Adirondacks

John E. Winkler

Edited by Linda Laing

North Country Books
Utica, New York

A CHERISHED WILDERNESS
The Adirondacks

ISBN 0-925168-59-9

Color Separations by
Rainbow Digicolor Inc., Toronto
Printed and bound in Hong Kong, China
By Book Art Inc., Toronto

First Printing 1998

Jacket front photo: Pond in the Silver Lake Wilderness Area, USGS *Three Ponds Mountain* quad – 1990

Page ii photo: View from Silver Lake Mountain, USGS *Redford, NY* quad – 1968

Jacket back photo: View from Giant Mountain, USGS *Elizabethtown* quad – 1978

Published by
NORTH COUNTRY BOOKS
311 Turner Street
Utica, New York 13501

Dedicated to
James A. Goodwin

Born in Hartford, Connecticut in 1910, Jim Goodwin has spent much of his life in Keene Valley, New York. He is a 46er, #24, and a member of the Adirondack Mountain Club.

Jim is a graduate of Williams College and Harvard University. As a teacher at Kingswood-Oxford School in West Hartford, Connecticut, he had summers free to lead various groups into the High Peaks as a professional as well as a volunteer guide. He also participated in the construction of many popular trails and worked with trail maintenance groups in the Adirondacks. He is a past chairman of the ADK Keene Valley Chapter and past president of the Adirondack Trail Improvement Society.

In the 1920s Jim came under the tutelage of John C. Case, a noted alpinist, who taught him the skills of rock climbing. He has climbed the cliffs on Indian Head, Wallface, Porter, Gothics and the Marcy Cliffs of Panther Gorge. He also has done a winter ascent of the now popular Colden Trap Dyke.

As a member of the Tenth Mountain Division during World War II, he taught rock climbing to soldiers for two years before going to Italy with the division.

Following the war, Jim, Fritz Weissner (a brilliant, advanced and dominant figure in rock climbing) and Hal Burton organized the first rock climbing school under the auspices of the Keene Valley Chapter of the ADK. In 1967 Jim, along with Trudy Healy, editor of the first ADK Rock Climbing Guide, organized and ran ADK's climbing school on Mount Jo.

Jim has been a valuable source of information for this book and also my companion book, *A Bushwhacker's View of the Adirondacks.*

EXPLORING THE SHANTY BROOK CLIFFS NEAR THE BLUE HILLS

Contents

Bald Peak, as seen from a vantage point south of its summit, after completing a bushwhack of Stevens Brook.

USGS *ELIZABETHTOWN* quad - 1978

Acknowledgments

Without help from others, this book would have been very difficult to do. I'd like to thank the following individuals and organizations for their contributions: Grace Hudowalski and the 46ers for allowing me access to the trailless peak log books and Jim Goodwin and Helen Menz for their stories on hiking in the 20s and 30s. James Papero, DEC Raybrook; David S. Larrabee, DEC Rodman; the Tug Hill Commission; the Tourist Information Center of Old Forge and the Saranac Lake Chamber of Commerce for their cooperation in answering my many questions.

I'd also like to thank Al Andrejcak, Kathleen Gill, Walt Hayes, Susan Roberts and Michael Whelan for accompanying me on hikes to obtain the many photos that appear in this book.

Five of the six pen and ink sketches and the one color pencil drawing were done by John Wiley. A member of the Schenectady Chapter of the ADK for twelve years and a 46er, he also designed the chapter's current patch. After living on the west coast for a few years, he currently resides with his wife, Elise Kessler Wiley, in Buckfield, Maine. He is a member of the Appalachian Mountain Club.

The pen and ink sketch on page 118 was drawn by a talented teenager, Michael Whelan. An honor student at Duanesburg Central School, he also plays the keyboard and drums. He is contemplating a career in either forestry or the arts or both and would like to travel to foreign countries. Mike has an interesting family background; his ancestors first came to America in 1634 from Holland. He is a descendant of Daniel Boone and Abraham Lincoln.

C. W. Uschman, a former neighbor and friend, wrote the four "ramblings" in this book. A Schenectady native, he worked for General Electric and the former ALCO Products before retiring on disability in 1947. He died in 1971 at the age of seventy.

Editor Linda Laing, an honors graduate of the State University of New York at Albany, is a technical writer and editor for the General Electric Company. She is also a freelance writer and author of *Guide to Adirondack Trails: Southern Region*, one of the Adirondack Mountain Club's Forest Preserve Series of guidebooks. Laing is a regular contributor to *Adirondack Life* magazine. A member of the ADK for over fifteen years, she is a 46er and has hiked the Northville-Lake Placid Trail end to end. She resides in Schenectady, New York.

View of Lake Placid and Mirror Lake from Little John Mountain.

USGS *SARANAC LAKE* quad - 1979

Introduction

My interest in the outdoors, especially in the woods and mountains, goes back to my childhood where I spent a considerable amount of time at my aunt's camp which was located in what is now Middle Grove State Park in Saratoga County. I took many walks through the woods, played in Frink Brook and, in late summer, picked many a quart of black thimble berries which were abundant in the area.

During the 1960s I made several trips to Heart Lake in the Adirondacks and climbed Mount Marcy and Mount McIntyre which is now known as Algonquin Peak. I also did many hikes in the East Stony Creek region, north of Northville.

In 1970, after coming home from two years in the Army, serving in Vietnam and Japan, I joined the Adirondack Mountain Club. It was from that time on that I began to do serious hiking. Eugene Brousseau, then an active ADK member, introduced me to bushwhacking and also gave me a lot of helpful hints on photography.

In 1976 I finished climbing all of the 46 High Peaks, with the help of many friends. Then I, in turn, helped others finish their climbs. Occasionally we would climb some by bushwhack routes. Later I decided to climb all 46 peaks without using trails or herd paths. It took about five years to bushwhack all the High Peaks. Many were horrendous climbs: Haystack, Colvin, the Sewards and Allen. Porter, Cascade, Phelps and even Marcy were some of the nicer, more pleasant bushwhacks.

Many friends have encouraged me to assemble a book of photos showing the Adirondacks from places most hikers never see, as over the years I had acquired many slides from my bushwhack adventures. In 1995 North Country Books published my first book, *A Bushwhacker's View of the Adirondacks*. It contains photos that were mostly in the High Peaks area, whereas this book contains photos from various parts of the Adirondacks as well as the High Peaks region.

To identify the location in which the photos were taken, a map reference line is given by each photo or group of photos. The maps quoted are the latest USGS 7.5 x 15 minute metric series, unless otherwise noted.

Many areas in the Adirondacks are private and one should obtain permission before hiking or bushwhacking on these privately owned lands.

About the Adirondacks

In 1916 New Yorkers, for the first time, authorized $10 million to be spent acquiring land for state park purposes. Since then more than $500 million has been appropriated through several Environmental Bond Acts to buy forest preserve land and wetlands, to create public campsites, to acquire stream rights and for public access.

In 1923 the first public campsite was constructed along the Sacandaga River near Wells. Today there are many such campsites throughout the Adirondack Park.

The Adirondack Park is the largest state park of its kind in the lower forty-eight states. It is a patchwork of public and private lands, with nearly 2.5 million acres now state-owned for public use. There are about 3,000 ponds and lakes, 1,500 miles of rivers and 2,000 miles of trails within the park. On seventeen of the highest peaks, from an elevation of approximately 4,500' and higher, are eighty-five acres classified as an Alpine Zone. This area is very similar to the Arctic Tundra where many rare alpine plants and wildflowers can be found. One must be very careful to stay on the marked trails in these areas because these delicate plants cannot survive if trampled on.

There are twelve counties within the Adirondack Park: Clinton, Essex, Franklin, Fulton, Hamilton, Herkimer, Lewis, Oneida, St. Lawrence, Saratoga, Warren and Washington. Essex and Hamilton are the only two counties that are completely within the blue line, an imaginary line indicating the boundary of the Adirondack Park. Hamilton County is also the least populated county in New York State. The eastern edge of the park is the most developed, and the central and western portions have the most ponds and lakes.

The hemlock tree is the Adirondacks' longest living tree, having a life span of about 600 years. The white pine is the tallest with a height of up to 125'. The gracious tamarack, a very slow growing pine, is the only northern conifer to completely shed all its needles in the fall. In October, before shedding, the tree turns a vibrant golden yellow.

Approximately sixty percent of New York State is forested. More forest land exists now than around the turn of the century, when uncontrolled lumbering took place causing soil erosion, floods and forest fires.

The highest body of water in the Adirondacks is Lake Tear of the Clouds at 4,345' between Mount Marcy and Mount Skylight. It is also the source of the Hudson River. A mile to the south, near Mount Redfield, is another high altitude pond, Moss Pond at 4,300'. Lake George is the largest lake in the Adirondacks that is entirely within the park. Lake Champlain, a portion of which is within the blue line, is the lowest elevation in the park, only 95' above sea level.

One hundred peaks in the Adirondacks range in height from 3,425' to 5,344', the latter being Mount Marcy, the state's highest mountain. It was first climbed in 1837 by a group of men led by Ebenezer Emmons, who was engaged in a geological survey for the state at the time. He named the mountain in honor of William L. Marcy, who was then the governor of the state.

While most of these mountains have trails, especially the first forty-six, many of the latter ones do not. But as more hikers take to the mountains, it's only a matter of time before most or all of these will have a trail or herd path on them as well.

Those unique three-sided log structures, popularly known as "Adirondack lean-tos," which are scattered throughout the wilderness areas, were first authorized by the Conservation Department in 1913. As of the mid-1990s, approximately 250 lean-tos were on state forest lands. To help protect the fragile ecology in the high elevations, all the lean-tos that were located over 3,500' in the High Peaks area were removed by the end of 1976.

Chapter One

Spring

SIMPLE SPRING BEAUTIES: GOLDTHREAD, BUNCHBERRY, CLINTONIA, WOOD SORREL

Were You There?

One fair day, in spring, I wander down a meadow lane,
O'er hill and dale, sprinting lightly like a deer,
No cares, no fears,
I witness the awakening of another season.

So once again, I journey on the soft earthy footpaths,
Over the hills, along the creeks and
Through the woodlands to commune
   with all that is Natural.

To rest beside the quiet pool,
To meditate and be thankful.

For beneath the cloud-studded blue sky,
In the shadow of tall pines,
Near the solidity of rock ledges,
Supping the wild berry and listening to the steady murmur
   of running waters,
I perceive a pattern and usefulness to it all.

I recognize in all these things,
The manifestation of a creative power,
Infinitely greater than just me.

C. W. Uschman

Opposite page:
Once much larger when beavers
had it dammed, this picturesque pond
is southeast of Roosevelt Hill.

USGS *NEWCOMB* quad - 1989

Photographed on the eastern slope of Boundary Peak, these hikers enjoy the last of the previous winter's snow. Mount Colden and Mount Marcy are in the background.

USGS *KEENE VALLEY* quad - 1979

Twin Pond.

An impressive view of Mount Colden, left, and Mount Marcy, right, from a shoulder of Calamity Mountain. The true summit is in the foreground.

USGS *SANTANONI PEAK* quad - 1979

A view of the High Peaks from the western shoulder of Macomb Mountain. Mount Marcy is in the center.

USGS *MOUNT MARCY* quad - 1979

MARSH MARIGOLDS (Buttercup family) - These beautiful golden yellow flowers are among the first wildflowers to bloom in the spring. They blossom in late April and early May in boggy areas and wetlands. Photographed near Minerva.

A view through the birches on a hill overlooking Joseph Pond.

USGS *NEWCOMB / DEERLAND* quads - 1989

In the Pharaoh Lake wilderness area this view to the north, overlooking Pyramid Lake, was taken from Bear Mountain.

Whitewater rafting in the spring is very popular here in the Hudson River Gorge.

USGS *DUTTON MOUNTAIN* quad - 1989

Between Hough Peak and South Dix is a 4,040' unnamed summit which has a nice rock slide on it. Since it does not lead to the popular peaks on either side of it, the slide is seldom climbed.

USGS **MOUNT MARCY** quad - 1979

Unnamed stream on MacNaughton Mountain's west side.

USGS *AMPERSAND LAKE* quad - 1978

A view of the Cedar River Flow is captured from Sugarloaf Mountain. Water-barrel Mountain is in the foreground.

USGS *BLUE MOUNTAIN / INDIAN LAKE* quads - 1989-90

Boreas River Gorge.

USGS *DUTTON MOUNTAIN* quad - 1989

Evidence of a blowdown several miles southeast of Sugarloaf Mountain while on a bushwhack to Panther Mountain.

USGS *BLUE MOUNTAIN LAKE / INDIAN LAKE* quads - 1989-90

Old tree stumps dot the shoreline of the Stillwater Reservoir in the west central region of the Adirondacks. This area is popular for wilderness shoreline camping, canoeing, boating, hunting, snowmobiling and cross country skiing. Photographed approximately one mile east of Hidden Lake Outlet.

USGS *STILLWATER / BEAVER RIVER* quads - 1989

A view of East Dix from Ledge Pond.

USGS *WITHERBEE* quad - 1978

SHINLEAF (Wintergreen family) - A rather common wildflower in the Adirondacks. It is found in June and has an average height of seven inches.

The Oswegatchie River above High Falls.

USGS *FIVE PONDS* quad - 1969

21

SPRING BEAUTIES (Purslane family) - Found in May, this small flower is quite attractive. It is commonly found in moist, open woodlands throughout the Adirondacks. In higher elevations it blooms much later in the season.

Gooseneck Pond as seen from trailless 1,850' Potter Mountain in the Pharaoh Lake Wilderness area.

USGS *GRAPHITE* quad - 1973

View of Whiteface from a shoulder of Kilburn Mountain.

USGS *LAKE PLACID* quad - 1979

Wilcox Lake.

USGS *HARRISBURG* quad - 1990

Outlet of Hot Water Pond flowing into Burroughs Cave.

Outlet of Hot Water Pond below Burroughs Cave. Polypody ferns grow mostly on rocks and are common throughout the Adirondacks and North America. They are usually less than a foot in height.

USGS *DUTTON MOUNTAIN* quad - 1989

This unique "knot" was photographed on the east side of Baldface Mountain.

USGS *DUTTON MOUNTAIN* quad - 1989

TROUT LILY, common in eastern North America in early spring, grows to a height of approximately ten inches and belongs to the Lily family.

26

View from trailless Red Rock Mountain.

USGS *LAKE PLACID / LEWIS* quads - 1979

Cellar Pond lies north of Cellar Mountain, a 3,447' peak which is 96th on the list of the one hundred highest Adirondack peaks.

USGS *WAKELY MOUNTAIN* quad - 1990

Chapter Two

Summer

SEARCHING THE HORIZON FROM THE "OTHER" NIPPLETOP MOUNTAIN

Summer, Idle Time

Relaxed, and lying comfortably on a soft
    carpet of dried pine needles in the shadow
    of a grove of tall monarchs;
Oblivious to most all sounds on this beautiful day,
Where all Nature seems to have paused in
    its striving purpose;
Where all growth, for the moment,
    appears to have reached its zenith,
    under the warmth of a mid-day sun.

Amid that quiet, hardly a disturbing influence,
    'nary a rustle is heard;
Only the soothing gurgle of a small brook,
    trickling relentlessly past
    moss covered stones;
There is a time for long thoughts—
Time for men to search their souls,
    and wonder—whether they've accomplished
    much by having done little or exerted
    plentifully and gathered adequate rewards.

C.W. Uschman

Just below the Hudson River Gorge, on the south side of the river, is Fox Hill. The view is looking south.

Tug Hill Plateau

Less than ten miles west of the Adirondack Park is a region called the Tug Hill Plateau. Due to its elevation (2,100' at its peak) and close proximity to Lake Ontario, the area averages fifty-five inches of precipitation annually. It is the snowiest and wettest area east of the Rocky Mountains.

On the plateau are numerous gulfs or gorges, two of which are partially or totally on state land and have access trails.

Inman Gulf is part of the 12,000-acre Tug Hill State Forest. Most of the land along the south rim is state owned, while most of the land along the north rim is private. It also has a fifty-foot waterfall, Rainbow Falls, which plunges into the gulf from the north rim. Most of this land was purchased in 1933 for $4 an acre.

Five miles south of Lowville, off Route 26, is the Whetstone Gulf. Completely protected as state land, this three-mile-long gorge has a trail system that circles the rim. A scenic recreation area since the 1800s, it also has over fifty campsites and a picnic and swimming area. This 2,100-acre park was developed in the 1930s by the New York State DEC and the federal CCC program.

Rocks containing fossils of shells and small sea creatures can be found in the stream beds of both gulfs.

A view from Inman Gulf's south rim. The gorge is 9½ miles long and 275' deep.

USGS *BARNES CORNERS / RODMAN* quads - 1959

A hiker inspects a land shift of the rocky, crumbly shale wall on Inman Gulf's eastern end, next to Rainbow Falls.

Whetstone Gulf from the south rim, photographed with an 18mm wide-angle lens.

While bushwhacking Algonquin from a point a mile north of Scotts Clearing, this nice view looking west was encountered. A shoulder of Street Mountain, as well as MacNaughton, Seymour and Donaldson Mountains are visible in the background.

USGS *KEENE VALLEY / AMPERSAND LAKE* quads - 1978-79

Blowdown from the July 1995 microburst storms which flattened 970,000 acres of forest. Photographed in July 1996 along the north shore of Lake Lila.

USGS *WOLF MOUNTAIN* quad - 1968

The Beaver River near Keepawa.

This view looking southwest from Frederick Mountain is a trailless peak west of Lake Lila and north of Nehasane Lake.

USGS *BEAVER RIVER* quad - 1989

View from Baldhead Mountain northwest of Stony Creek, New York.

39

Three beautiful ponds are found on the south side of Three Ponds Mountain in the Silver Lake Wilderness area in the southern Adirondacks. This is a view of the first pond.

USGS *THREE PONDS MOUNTAIN* quad - 1990

40

Birch bark in the late afternoon sun, photographed near Cedar River.

Southwestern shore of Lake Lila.

USGS *BEAVER RIVER* quad - 1989

O.K. Slip Falls, near the Hudson River Gorge, is the Adirondacks' highest falls at 190'.

USGS *DUTTON MOUNTAIN* quad - 1989

BUTTERFLY WEED - This very showy member of the milkweed family blooms during July and August in sandy areas and along roadsides. It is a protected species in New York State.

COMMON MILKWEED (Milkweed family) - This plant blooms in late July and early August in fields and open areas. The Monarch butterfly enjoys the nectar of the blooms.

ORANGE HAWKWEED (Sunflower family) - These and the yellow hawkweeds are extremely common throughout the Adirondacks, and are found almost everywhere in mid-summer. Photographed close-up with an 18mm lens, they make a striking picture.

SUNDEWS (Sundew family) - This protected species is found in bogs, blooms in mid-summer and is insectivorous. Photographed at Lens Lake.

USGS *HARRISBURG* quad - 1990

Bullhead Pond Brook Falls southwest of Venison Mountain.

USGS *DUTTON MOUNTAIN* quad - 1989

Pond along Beaver Brook, east of Snowy Mountain.

USGS *INDIAN LAKE* quad - 1990

A mountain meadow near Benz Pond two miles southeast of Azure Mountain, an old fire tower peak.

This tree once grew atop an old stump which has since rotted away. Photographed in the Sawtooth Mountains.

Many rocky cliffs like this are found on Mount Carl, west of Pokomoonshine Mountain.

USGS *AuSABLE FORKS* quad - 1978

Deerfield Mountain as seen from a shoulder of Mount Carl.

Pokomoonshine Mountain has a superb view of Lake Champlain and Camel's Hump Mountain in Vermont. The mountain's south and east sides have many cliffs which are very popular with rock climbers.

The Oswegatchie River and the blowdown from the 1995 microburst, southeast of High Falls in the Five Ponds Wilderness Area.

An ADK trail crew works on the High Falls Trail south of Wanakena. This area was the hardest hit during the 1995 microburst. By 1997 much of the area had new growth, including many berry bushes, which will provide birds, bears and other animals with a good food source for many years. Such storms are natural and do have beneficial side effects.

From Sugarloaf Mountain, a fine view of the High Peaks far to the north.

USGS *BLUE MOUNTAIN LAKE* quad - 1989

Sawtooth Mountains

In the northwest sector of the Adirondack High Peaks region, the Sawtooth Mountains area is the largest trailless section, covering nearly 22,000 acres or thirty-four square miles. Five of the peaks pictured here are on the list of the one hundred highest Adirondack peaks and range in height from 3,460' to 3,877'. Along the eastern edge, near Averyville, are a number of old logging roads and hunters' trails which give some access to this rugged and remote region.

This bog, southeast of Alford Mountain near the east branch of Cold Brook, was photographed during the drought of 1995. Note the dry moss and low water in the stream channel.

USGS *AMPERSAND LAKE* quad - 1978

A view looking north along Vanderwhacker Brook.

USGS *NEWCOMB* quad - 1989

Rock Climbing

The Adirondacks are very attractive to rock climbers. Many of the High Peaks, with their anorthosite rock, have slides on them. Among the most popular are those on East Dix, Dix, Giant, Nippletop, Wright Peak, Whiteface and the east side of Colden Mountains.

In the southern region Roger's Rock, Moxam Dome and Crane Mountain are popular climbs. In the northern region locations such as Chapel Pond, Cascade Lakes, Pokomoonshine, Big Slide Mountain, Wallface Mountain and the west side of Mount Colden attract climbers. In all there are approximately eight hundred fifty routes not including variations or slide climbs.

The climbing routes in the Adirondacks have very "colorful" names attached to them. *No Comments from the Peanut Gallery, Flying and Drinking and Drinking and Driving, Pete's Wicked Flail, Till the Fat Lady Sings, Five Hundred Rednecks with Guns, Holiday in Cambodia* and *Potato Chip Flake* are just some of the fascinating names they have acquired.

Near the summit of Indian Pass, adjacent to Wallface Mountain, there are several small ice caves where snow and ice can be found as late as August. There are many other caves throughout the Adirondacks. One is near Chapel Pond, below the Giant's Washbowl, another can be found in Panther Gorge and still another on the east shore of the Lower Ausable Lake, at the base of Mount Colvin, although it is located on private property and is not accessible to the public.

Rock climbing is very popular on Pokomoonshine Mountain.

USGS *AUSABLE FORKS* quad - 1978

The "trap dyke" on Mount Colden makes for a nice rock scramble and is a popular ice climb in winter as well.

USGS *KEENE VALLEY* quad - 1979

A rock scrambler on Wilmington Notch Mountain. Whiteface Mountain is in the background.

USGS *LAKE PLACID* quad - 1979

A still water section of East Stony Creek about two miles northwest of Bakertown.

USGS *HARRISBURG* quad - 1990

A view from the top of the Bottle Slide on Giant Mountain.

Chapter Three

Autumn

HEADING SOUTH OVER HARRINGTON MOUNTAIN POND

October Impression

Come, for a jaunt with me,
    Up into the hills,
    Out of the closed valleys
    Amid the glories of autumn.

To witness an encore of Nature's manifestations
    atop the rolling hillslopes,
    Where the grasses have faded,
    The green foliage changed to a
    multitudinous coloration;
    The Oak leaves a rustic brown,
    The Sugar Maple a scarlet red,
    And the Tamarack display their
    yellowed boughs,
    Clinging tenaciously in one final showing.

A gorgeous sunset illuminates the
    advancing clouds,
    To reveal unforgettable shades of
    red, yellow, orange and purple;
    In a slowly changing spectrum—
    A sight forever impressed upon
    the receptive mind.

'Tis Nature's farewell gesture to the
    ending of another cycle,
    In the ever-changing pattern
    In the scheme of things.

Then the shadows lengthen,
    The light begins to fade
    And the last wandering bird
    finds its night's resting place.

There is a hush, an almost eerie silence.
    Strange forms appear on the darkened rocks.

The long slender blue-gray clouds
    stretching across the horizon,
    Become obscured and mingle with the
    general overcast,
    And the fast approaching darkness.

Here, then, is peace and quiet,
    Along the slow running brooks,
    In the nearly naked woodlands.

Little lights flickering throughout the valley
    begin jumping into prominence;
    Indicate that here, too,
    There is reconciliation in the
    hearts and souls of men.

All things, spiritual and living,
    Must have purpose and destiny.
In this one glorious moment of Autumn splendor,
    Mankind is humbled by it all.

C.W. Uschman

Opposite page:
Photographed with an 18mm lens, both
Elk Lake and Clear Pond are captured in
one picture from Sunrise Mountain.

USGS **MOUNT MARCY** quad - 1979

A view of Wilmington Notch Mountain and the cliffs on an unnamed mountain between Sunrise Notch and Moss Cliff.

USGS *LAKE PLACID* quad - 1979

Reflection

Everything on this earth, and in the Universe,
is interrelated—

    My brothers—the beasts,
    My sisters—the winds,
    The snow—the rain,
    The cold—the heat,
    The sun—the moon,
    The stars and the distant planets.

That Force responsible for our creation
    also provided the means for our
    substance and survival.

Man formulates his plans;

Nature's are so much more comprehensive
    and inspiring.

                  C.W. Uschman

East inlet stream, Elk Lake.

USGS **MOUNT MARCY** quad - 1979

Brilliant autumn foliage on the south shoulder of Dutton Mountain.

USGS *DUTTON MOUNTAIN* quad - 1989

Mount Dix and Nippletop as seen from a bog north of Beech Ridge.

USGS *MOUNT MARCY* quad - 1979

Fall foliage at its peak. Photo taken along an old logging road near the base of Merrills Hill.

USGS *SCHROON LAKE* quad - 1979

Autumn splendor at Boreas River Gorge.

USGS *DUTTON MOUNTAIN* quad - 1989

Brown Pond.

USGS *INDIAN LAKE* quad - 1990

Northeast of Jerry Vly is this beaver pond at an elevation of 1,557'.

Fall foliage on Pine Hill.

USGS *SCHROON LAKE* quad - 1979

NEW ENGLAND ASTER (Sunflower family) - Growing to a height of about five feet, this is one of the most colorful of the autumn flowers. It is found in moist meadows and open areas.

Bartlett Pond on the southeast shoulder of McKenzie Mountain.

Hoffman and Niagara Mountains are seen from an unnamed peak of 3,410' southeast of Macomb.

Merrills Hill from Alder Brook at the height of the fall foliage.

USGS *SCHROON LAKE* quad - 1979

A rock slide formed in October 1995 on the shoulder of Kilburn Mountain. Photographed from an old beaver meadow near the base.

USGS *LAKE PLACID* quad - 1979

With an elevation of only 2,484', Seymour Mountain, near Averyville, has a pleasant view from its mostly rocky summit. Alford Pond is in the foreground.

USGS *SARANAC LAKE* quad - 1979

Autumn woods on the north side of Seymour Mountain.

West of Schroon Lake there are a number of "hills" which are trailless and have excellent views. This view of Schroon Lake was photographed from Pine Hill.

USGS *SCHROON LAKE* quad - 1989

Found throughout most of eastern North America, growing to a height of ten to fifteen feet, the WITCH HAZEL (Witch Hazel family) blooms in the fall after shedding its leaves.

Late autumn woods near Murphy Lake. Rand Mountain can be seen through the trees.

USGS *HOPE FALLS* quad - 1990

Fall foliage on Rand Mountain.

A view from McKenzie Mountain near Lake Placid. This is also a fine view of the Kilburn Mountain rock slide.

USGS *SARANAC LAKE* quad - 1979

Harrisburg Lake in October.

USGS *HARRISBURG* quad - 1990

Autumn woods and an unnamed stream between Venison and Dutton Mountains.

USGS *DUTTON MOUNTAIN* quad - 1989

A superb view of Macomb, Wyman, East Dix and Spotted Mountains from Gui Pond.

USGS *WITHERBEE* quad - 1978

Callahan Pond.

USGS *SCHROON LAKE* quad - 1989

Bog south of Fullers, adjacent to East Stony Creek.

Chapter Four

Winter

SNOWY MOUNTAIN VIEW FROM SQUAW MOUNTAIN

Wintertime Lament

In summer, when the sun is hot,
  and sweat trickles down my brow,
I dream of frolicking in the deep snow,
The tougher the goin', the greater the sport,
Trippin' over fallen branches, pant legs frozen stiff,
  and fingers numbed by the cold.
At six below, nary a bird in the sky,
This is the life, out under the clear blue.

Where the whistling wind blows like fury,
  and the snowbanks glisten and give challenge,
  to race and run o'er the hard packed crusts.

The trees are bare, the sand hard as a rock,
  the chirping warblers gone,
  and the furred animals take sheltered refuge.

But then, as the summer blossoms wither,
I too, am a bit older now, and the wintry
  blasts send tingly shudders up and down
  my aging spine.

There comes then, thoughts of warmer doin's,
  'cause this rugged stuff for me now is naught.

Until another time, I think and realize,
  the wanderings wide, were occasionally rough
  and quite enough!

C. W. Uschman

Opposite page:
View from Silver Lake Mountain.
USGS *REDFORD* quad - 1968

Early winter snowfall east of Railroad Notch.

USGS *KEENE VALLEY* quad - 1979

Photographed in January at Auger Falls, these artistic ice designs change completely every few days.

USGS *HARRISBURG / WELLS* quads - 1990

Ice laden trees atop Auger Falls.

A view looking north from 1,500' Moose Mountain near Wells.

USGS *THREE PONDS MOUNTAIN / WELLS* quads - 1990

Near the summit of Porter Mountain in January.

Catamount Mountain as seen from its lower shoulder.

USGS *WILMINGTON* quad - 1978

Mount Dix from Rhododendron Pond.

USGS *WITHERBEE* quad - 1978

Snowshoeing between Morgan Mountain and Cooper Kiln Pond.

USGS *WILMINGTON* quad - 1978

Northeast end of Long Lake, south of Otter Lake, in the western Adirondacks.

Only 2,225' in elevation, Harris Hill has three open summits with excellent views. Shown here is a fine view of the Dix Range from the north summit.

USGS *WITHERBEE* quad - 1978

Goodnow Pond as seen from a viewpoint looking southwest from Goodnow Mountain. On its summit is a fire tower renovated by staff and students of the State College of Forestry.

USGS *NEWCOMB* quad - 1978

Icy trees on the southeast side of Giant Mountain.

USGS *ELIZABETHTOWN* quad - 1978

Rondaxe Mountain, shown on the map as Bald Mountain, has a nice view of the Chain Lakes. Blue Mountain can be seen in the far background.

USGS *OLD FORGE* quad - 1989

100

Birches in Middle Grove State Forest.

USGS *MIDDLE GROVE* quad - 1967

Winter wonderland on Pitchoff Mountain.

USGS *Keene Valley* quad - 1979

Algonquin, Boundary and Iroquois Peaks as seen from Wallface Ponds.

A pristine winter wonderland seen from Marcy Plateau. Little Marcy is in the background.

Boreas River northeast of Route 28N.

USGS *NEWCOMB / BLUE RIDGE* quads - 1989

Mountain Memories

In the northern Adirondacks there are more than 2,000 mountains, but the most popular and well-known are those of 4,000' or more in height. In 1948 an organization called "The Adirondack Forty-Sixers" was founded. Any person who had climbed the forty-six Adirondack peaks over 4,000' could join. Today there are over 4,000 members.

In the first half of the nineteenth century, twenty-four of the popular forty-six had no trails and herd paths were unheard of. They were true bushwhacks in every sense of the word. Jim Goodwin, who finished his first round of the forty-six peaks in 1940 and is 46er #24, recalled climbing Mount Marcy in 1919 and the only people on the trail were members of his climbing party. Jim also was on Mount Marcy in 1928 with his sister, Peggy O'Brien, who was chairwoman at Johns Brook Lodge for many years and they watched the construction of the MacDonald Storm Shelter. This was a stone "lean-to" constructed on the summit of Marcy which was to provide shelter to hikers caught there in bad weather.

Pirie MacDonald, president of the Adirondack Mountain Club at the time, had the shelter constructed with permission of the Conservation Department. At a cost of $2,500, he financed the project himself. He also designed it so it blended in with the natural surroundings. It faced the southeast towards Mount Haystack and was just below the highest point on the mountain. The shelter had doors to keep out the cold winds. The back wall was the natural summit rock of Marcy so it officially was a lean-to! Jim Goodwin recalls spending many nights in that lean-to; one in particular was a Christmas Eve when temperatures in Keene Valley registered 10° below zero.

The lean-to was in good shape until 1942, but after returning home from the war in 1945, Jim found it in disrepair. The lean-to was entirely dismantled in the early 1960s.

Jim Goodwin recalls his hiking experiences in the 1920s:

Nearly everybody used ponchos purchased from army surplus stores after World War I for rain gear. A few people sported Abercrombie and Fitch rain suits, but these were excessively hot. (Gortex was not developed until late in this century.)

We did have Ever-Ready flashlights, but their batteries were comparatively weak by today's standards, and didn't last long. A lot of us used lanterns made from tin cans into which candles would be stuck at right angles to the opening, a wire served as a handle. Some people used carbide lamps which, with water dripping into the calcium carbide particles, furnished a gas for long-lasting and powerful practical light.

Traveling to the Adirondacks in the early part of the century was much different than with today's modern cars and highways. People would take the train to Lake Placid or Westport and then take horse-drawn wagons to their destinations.

By the late teens horse travel was passé and the automobile served as transportation, except during the winter when unplowed roads made travel by car nearly impossible.

Many of the early roads were gravel and a trip to the Adirondacks took twice as long as it does today. Jim Goodwin recalls that a trip from Hartford, Connecticut to Keene Valley in the late 1920s took fifteen hours in a Model T Ford. It had two forward speeds and a cruising speed of 35 mph.

Helen Menz, who is 46er #42 and finished her first round of the forty-six on Allen in 1946, has this to say about hiking in the 1930s:

On our first trip up Mount Marcy, in the spring of 1932, our equipment was primitive to say the least. My sister, Mary Dittmar (wife of Dr. A. Dittmar, Executive Secretary for the 46ers), and I had packbaskets. We had gone hunting and snowshoeing with our Dad so we had some Bean-type boots as well. Most of our Girl Scout friends had shoes with rubbers or rubber boots. The rubbers and boots had a tendency to get lost in the deep mud that was on the trail. At that point a search would go on, probing the mud to find them. There were many such spots on the trail because of the recent rain and snow. There were no bridges or stepping stones on the trail, so often we took off our boots to wade the streams.

We had no sleeping bags. Everyone rolled up blankets, the approved Girl Scout way. Each slide in the mud could mean lost footgear, wet bedroll and a wet seat! Except for our packbaskets, the packs were a variety of soft Boy Scout packs, which had no pockets for storing small items and had very little room. Things often would get lost in the bottoms of these packs. We used newspaper to insulate under our blankets in the lean-to as well as to help start a fire. Candles were also used in starting fires and for light in the lean-to at night. Tin cans made a good safe candle holder and created more light because of the reflection.

Our food was mostly canned goods. We had a milk substitute which was always lumpy. Our cooking was done in "beer buckets," which were thin tin buckets with wire handles. These buckets were supposedly used to bring beer home from the nearest saloon, hence the name. We used these for years, being careful to dry them well so they would not rust at the seams.

We would cook on a wood fire; since there weren't many people in the mountains then, wood was easy to find. Most lean-tos had a small pile of dry wood inside. It was left by thoughtful hikers in case others came to the lean-to in the rain or at night.

We met only one person on the trail during the entire trip. It was not necessary to pack a heavy tent as there always was ample room in the lean-tos, which were mostly empty.

A few years later we moved to Albany. The Albany Chapter of ADK taught us how to make our own sleeping bags. Some people even sewed zippers into the bag. We bought a bolt of balloon silk, which was almost white, not a good color for camping in the Adirondacks. When the right amount of material was cut from the bolt, it was dyed. We all helped each other change the color of the material. Most of which turned out to be many shades of brown. A few people opted for green.

The four layers of material were sewed in a proper shape for adding the fill, which was three pounds of wool batting. There were two layers on the bottom and one on top.

Tying parties were held and everyone helped tie the wool batting in place with woolen yarn. The finished bags were then sewed up for the last time. These bags were used for many years. We could stuff them in our packs very well. Many years later the fill was so flat that it was no longer warm enough and we went to the new fiberfill bags.

We now had a nice light material to help keep us dry. We purchased oiled silk to use as a vapor barrier while camping, but have no idea now where we got it.

Of the forty-six peaks, twenty (plus MacNaughton) are considered "trailless." These peaks have canisters approved by the DEC on their summits, which not only define the summit, but also allow people to record their names and comments.

The first peak to receive one of the official canisters was East Dix, on October 14, 1949. Twelve years later the last canister was installed on MacNaughton on August 15, 1961. Prior to the 46ers' canisters, there were a number of homemade ones which date back to 1946. They were not always placed at the highest point.

The log books contain nostalgia, experiences and even some historical information the hikers experienced on their climbs. Over the years some of the log books were lost and not all indicate the date the first official canister was installed.

As part of the DEC's High Peaks Wilderness Area Unit Management Plan, the canisters on the summits of the "trailless" peaks will eventually be eliminated.

What follows are a few comments from each of the twenty-four peaks which had or have canisters on their summits as of 1997.

SANTANONI PEAK (First official canister placed July 5, 1957)

6/23/60

Two of us up from Duck Hole. BLACK FLIES STRONG. Marcy just visible in mist. Warm, partly cloudy.

R.B. - Rochester, N.Y.

7/13/62

Brush was very wet on way up, we're soaked to the skin, but no farther! 43 on 4th round.

T.H.

10/4/68

Taking old book out to Grace—its full. Snow and sleet at 3,800' elev. Fortunately shower type and ground is warm, but hands numb. Can hardly write. Had to come back today to retrieve a pack for one of our group, left behind yesterday on account of time lost with herd paths on the Couchy-Santanoni ridge. This is no backpackers paradise.

M.T.I.

PANTHER PEAK (First official canister placed July 6, 1961)

8/18/61

The view is beautiful - I have exposed too much film and I will never find the money to develop it.

T.G.

Is the above a hint father should come across?

J.G.

8/14/75

What's a herd path?

B.W. & J.W. - Scotia, N.Y.

6/10/83

Late to bed, late to rise, the sun was bright, the clouds were high. Fantastic day for Santanoni viewing, but late in the day, we said nothing doing. Will try again on a bright sunny day - hope the rain clouds will stay away. Have fun, everyone.

G.P. & L.F. - Glens Falls, N.Y.

COUCHSACHRAGA PEAK

9/14/86

#45 and my last trailless peak. If you see some lunatic on top of Haystack in a powder blue tuxedo, be kind, it will be my 28th birthday (Sep. 26, 1986) and my 46th Peak!!

J.G. - Albany, N.Y.

6/26/90

Couch reminds me of the Energizer Rabbit - Just keeps on going, and going, and going and going . . .

B. & D.H.

STREET MOUNTAIN

Ascended what we thought to be Nye. But the pundits say its Street, June 9, 1955. On to Nye - wish it were Nigher.

P.F.J.   G.E.M. - Canton, N.Y.

7/6/62

Dear 46ers: Where the hell were the herd paths on Street? They must have been made for pygmies.

The Rondacks are a place where Nature has bestowed her benevolent hand upon all those who attempt to climb her mighty peaks.

M.P. & K.B.

NYE (First official canister placed May 30, 1953)

7/27/59

The hikers arrive on well-trodden feet, they sit on silent haunches, Looking over flies and blowdown. And then they plod home.

J.O'B. M.S. & M.S. (with help from Carl Sandberg)

7/4/76

Happy Birthday America.

P.R. & H.R. - Keene Valley, N.Y.

GRAY PEAK

8/2/88

Hot, Hot, Hot, and bugs too!

R.C. - Schenectady, N.Y.

8/24/94

Great day, sunny, high 70s, nice views! On to Skylight, then Cliff and Redfield tomorrow. 46er's here we come!

M.E. & M.E.

IROQUOIS PEAK (Canister removed in September of 1976)

5/15/73

Left Adirondac Loj 12:30 a.m., almost a full moon. Top of Algonquin 3:30 a.m. Windy and cold. Numb fingers. WHAT A SUNRISE!

T.S. & D.E.

6/12/76

Mother Nature here I am again. Opened by your beauty;
When I look, I can see afar.
And I feel my freedom's up to par.
Up, down, all around, the hills are rolling,
and I'll be back for another showing.

A.J.Y. - Watertown, N.Y.

ROCKY PEAK (First peak to have canister removed, May 28, 1968)

7/9/61

This peak is not trailless, there is a trail from Giant and two hunters trails—one on the SE side, one on the NE side. The bugs are bad, simply awful! Sure beats Bear Mountain, NY.

J.D. L.D. M.D. & R.D.

8/25/65

31st peak!!! Am now an aspiring, inspiring, perspiring and tired 46er! To JBL tonight to meet Dad.

J.V.K. - Reading Center, N.Y.

REDFIELD (First official canister placed May 1953)

5/31/76

For the first time Allen looks like more than just some rings on a topo map. Nice view.

T.K. - Cazenovia, N.Y.

8/3/88

Everyone should try bushwhacking from Allen to Redfield with full packs - don't forget the cheese! How's it going Whippoorwill? What's cookin' good lookin'? Let's meet at the Barnstead for a beer.

J.Z. - St. Louis

CLIFF MOUNTAIN

6/27/75

This has to be the worst mountain I've been on.

D.S.

4/5/76

As the great conqueror Atilla the Hun might have said - "God I'm glad we brought the Champagne!" Unfortunately we didn't.

T.W.S. - Middlebury, Vt.

ALLEN (First official canister placed September 19, 1953)

The following 4 members of the AMC New York Chapter reached the summit of Allen at 3:00 pm on Sept. 1, 1946. This is our 45th peak - only Phelps to go.

S.B.
A.B.
P.C.
P.K.

1/24/65

Excuse handwriting, colder than ah, er . . . down below. Left Stillwater 7:00 a.m. arrived on top 12:30 - 3 feet snow, drifts, powder and windy up here - bye, bye -

W.C. C.B. - Keene Valley, N.Y.

7/20/91

Dear Abbey, Dear Abbey,
She could have told,
We'd be 46er's before we're that old,
The hiking, the climbing, it's not hard to believe,
Just ask our feet, ankles and knees.

B. & G.D. - Red Creek, N.Y.

MacNAUGHTON (Official canister placed August 15, 1961)

9/4/75

Who ever said this was the middle peak had too much to drink or was a Sierra Club member who never climbed it. We came up from Wallface Ponds. F.R. came across a log. I fell in and had to climb up from the bottom of the creek with a wet _____ ! You fall in and figure how wet I was!

G.B. - Clifton Park, N.Y.

6/12/76

Up from Wallface Ponds. Didn't find "herd path," so just climbed, it didn't take long to get to the summit, but it took 50 minutes to find the canister. Thank God - Beautiful day.

D.L. - Tupper Lake, N.Y.

ESTHER

3/30/62

Skiing up wasn't hard, but how will we ever get down this mashed potato snow?

T.H.

6/9/73

In spite of rain, snow, hail and Bugs!

P.R.

PHELPS MOUNTAIN (Canister removed July 1971)

8/15/63

If this is a "trailless peak" then Blake, Yard, Lower Wolf Jaw and Colvin are peakless trails!

C.K. - Teaneck, N.J.

8/21/67

Whoopee - we're here - no matter that I'm nearly fagged out, that we nearly caused a mudalanche, that the pack nearly crushed me - we're here, praise the Gremlins. Keep the faith baby (I mean Katonah!)

G.S.

TABLETOP (First official canister placed June 4, 1959)

8/9/90

Mostly cloudy, brisk winds, warm and damn buggy. All the black flies have retired and moved to this summit. ~~TABLETOP~~ BUGTOP

T.D. - Montreal, Que.

8/25/85

This is a miserable mountain with no view, hardly any rock, hardly any trail, and a stupid name.

D.A.

MARSHALL (First official canister placed May 30, 1958)

8/11/66

Got up here and we're soaked. Opened the pack for the jelly and found it had broken and jelly was squishing all over the place. So we ended up eating retarded wheat thins. ♪ I'll ♪ see ♪ you in September. ♪

B.D.

6/3/67

I'm eating my lunch and the flies are eating me.

N.D. #46

7/20/67

2 years ago I led 8 other boys up the backside of Iroquois while trying to climb Marshall. It's nice to look from Marshall to Iroquois for a change.

J.H.

MACOMB (First official canister placed October 10, 1958)

8/24/52

No Elk in Elk Lake

No Giants on Giant

No Basins on Basin

No riders on Saddleback.

F.S.C.

8/24/85

Raining and freezing half to death - came up the wrong slide (the one to the north) now off to South and East Dix. I WANNA BE A 46ER!!

T.E. - Lake George

9/8/90

It has been an excellent day. Finally we have reached our destination - Macomb. 5 peaks today, it's great! Now we can hike down to Lillian Brook where cold Genny Cream awaits us. BOY, COULD I GO FOR A GENNY NOW!

S.P. - Boonville, N.Y.

EAST DIX (First official canister placed October 14, 1949)

5/27/84

The thrill of victory, is the agony of de feet.

D.M. - Hamlin, N.Y.

8/19/93

Going for Hough, then maybe Dix. 1:00 p.m. and we've done three peaks already.
Roses are red, violets are blue,
These mountains are the best God could do.

B.H. - Hudson Falls, N.Y.

HOUGH MOUNTAIN (First official canister placed August 17, 1956)

8/4/62

All I wanted to do was get home from Dix - but somehow I ended up here. So I figured I better sign my name.

B.C. - Manlius, N.Y.

9/9/76

Well, first we walked straight and then we turned right and went up a lot. Then we went up lots more, and then we stopped. Then we walked flat and then we walked down a lot. Boy, did we walk down a lot, and then we walked up some and now we're here.

J.F. #24

9/28/95

Warm in the bush,
Cool on the rocks,
Color on the leaves,
Blisters in my socks.

J.G. - Albany, N.Y.

SOUTH DIX

5/24/84

Weather: It tends to be scattered.

J.L. T.P. P.W. &K.O. - Pompey, N.Y.

9/1/84

He who stays in the Bouquet River Valley shall never get over the hill.

T.B. - Niskayuna Warrior

MOUNT SEYMOUR (First official canister placed September 30, 1958)

8/23/74

BUGS!!! Ych!   J.R.
BUGS!   H.D.
BUGS!!   D.W.R.

9/4/77

Breathtaking, no people! Party of three. Fools names, and fools faces, always appear in public places.

R.C. C.D. &D.S.

6/23/94

Thank God I'm alive and not decomposing in the backwoods without a clue. Started bushwhacking like an idiot at the dirt road. From there it was half-assed cliffs, until I hit the false summit. But then I found this trail like a dream. Praise the Lord.

J.R. #35

P.S. This was my H.S. graduation present to myself. HA!

SEWARD MOUNTAIN

9/6/66

Good bushwhack from Rondeau's. Damn clouds got here same time I did 3:30 p.m.

T.A.H. - Vestal, N.Y.

7/13/79

T.C. Park Ranger NYSDEC Saranac Lake
Congratulations R.B. if you've already been to Seymour. If not, don't bushwhack straight over, it's insane. Mr. Goodwin was right!

DONALDSON MOUNTAIN

8/2/70

Went over Donaldson accidentally on way to Emmons.

G.R. G.W.

8/29/72

MADE IT - Huge black furry animal with claws and teeth followed us but disappeared right before here. Gorgeous view.

P.W.

8/9/78

Risking life and limb through the dark and dreaded forest of Ni. beware of the mud monsters.

D.S. & A.C.

EMMONS MOUNTAIN (First official canister placed September 3, 1950)

8/8/56

8:00 p.m. sun time. Sun about to set. Have spent all day getting here. Left Ward Brook lean-to 7:00 a.m. Seward was comparatively easy. Climbed a subsidiary peak of Seward (the rocky one) thinking it was Donaldson. (I didn't believe the map.) Then was on all peaks of Donaldson and found only an upside-down rusty tin can. We couldn't turn down to the Cold River Valley with Emmons so close, so here we are. Sun is a beautiful orange. What are we gonna do now?

G.S. C.S. M.S. & E.S.

8/27/77

On to Seymour! Didn't bring a machete, so I'll have to use my teeth!!

J.F.

The trailless High Peaks are not the only place log books have been placed. Many of the Adirondack 100 highest mountains have homemade canisters and record books on their summits, and some lean-tos have them as well, which are placed there by the lean-to caretakers. Below is an excerpt taken from the log book at Murphy Lake lean-to (USGS *HOPE FALLS* quad - 1990). It was placed there by Brian Wetmore, the lean-to steward (1994-1996).

MURPHY LAKE LEAN-TO

10/19/96

On our travels through this rugged land we encountered many perilous dangers and many more surprises. First as we crossed from the tundra in the north to this woodland we were followed by a pack of blood thirsty white wolves. Luckily for the ice chasm we escaped their deadly incisors. Next we ran into the cave bear on Delif's Point. That was a nasty event. We attempted to surround it, but it wasn't very dumb and got hold of poor Robert, tearing him from limb to limb! By the time we reached Middle Lake we had run out of supplies and our rations had been gone for a week. Already four have died of the cold and Tucker has gone mad, and thinks he's an elf. I am the last sane one of our small expedition. If anyone finds this and I have passed away, please make sure this story reaches the outside world. Let our story be told, so that we did not pass away into the void of time.

M.E.

12/28/96

I wonder how much Irish Coffee it took to get this great saga in the book?

K.G. - Schenectady, N.Y.

Clubs and Organizations

There are numerous clubs and organizations concerned with protecting and preserving the Adirondacks, not just local organizations, but national ones as well. The ones listed below represent a diversified range of goals and/or are ones that I am affiliated with.

The Adirondack Council. This is an 18,000-member, privately funded, not-for-profit organization which was formed in 1975. It is the state's leading environmental advocacy organization working to protect and enhance the natural and human communities of New York State's six-million-acre Adirondack Park—the most spectacular wilderness and open space reserve east of the Mississippi River. The Council's work includes: 1) educating the public, policymakers, and representatives of the news media on the conservation needs of the Park; 2) monitoring, aiding, encouraging, and prodding state government; 3) mobilizing public opinion when major threats and opportunities arise; 4) undertaking research and policy analysis; and 5) pursuing action when needed.

The Council's member organizations include: *The Association for the Protection of the Adirondacks, Citizens Campaign for the Environment, National Audubon Society, National Parks and Conservation Association, Natural Resources Defense Council*, and *The Wilderness Society*, with combined memberships of more than 1.4 million people.

The Association for the Protection of the Adirondacks. At the start of the 20th century a young Adirondack Park faced many threats. Lumbering, forest fires, dams and commercial development all threatened the forest preserve. As a result the first citizens' organization for the Adirondacks, *The Association for the Protection of the Adirondacks*, was created in 1901. It will celebrate its centennial anniversary in the year 2001.

The Adirondack 46ers. This is a non-profit organization whose members have climbed the major forty-six peaks of the Adirondacks. It is dedicated to environmental protection, to education for proper usage of wilderness areas, and participates in work projects, in conjunction with the DEC, to meet these objectives.

In May of 1948 a group of Adirondack climbers met at Adirondak Loj to discuss forming a hiking club for those who had climbed and those who were interested in climbing the "46." The group was orgnaized under the leadership of President Grace Hudowalski and Treasurer Adolf Dittmar. Over the last fifty years the organization's numbers have increased from fifty-four to over 4,000 members.

From a small number of dedicated climbers joining to share a common hobby and bond, the group has developed into a dedicated band of environmentally aware and proactive "mountain stewards." For them, the CHERISHED WILDERNESS deserves and requires preservation, maintenance, education and, most importantly, a "watchful eye and a strong voice."

Working in cooperation with the DEC and other interested groups, the 46ers have fostered the stewardship concept through sponsoring various activities while supporting the efforts of other individuals and clubs. Each year over one thousand hours of volunteer trail work is organized by the 46er Trailmasters and each May over fifty participants attend the "Outdoor Leadership Workshop." In the past the 46ers have joined in litter removal activities, distributed litter bags and trowels and helped finance the Ridge Runner and Summit Steward efforts. Currently, in conjunction with the ADK and DEC, rehabilitation of the herd paths on trailless peaks has started. In an effort to steer climbers to more environmentally sound routes and to decrease the number of search and rescue missions, a committee has begun to modify and reroute wilderness paths in an effort to maintain the wilderness experience while enhancing safety and minimizing impact.

For the thousands of active members, the slogan "Climbing Partners, Mountain Stewards" has served to define the 46ers' philosophy and direction. They, too, "cherish" the Adirondacks and work to preserve its resources.

Adirondack Mountain Club (ADK). Headquartered in Lake George, New York, ADK is a non-profit organization dedicated to conservation, education and recreation in New York State. Founded in 1922, ADK has more than 22,000 members in its twenty-six chapters. Club activities include hiking, biking, canoeing, backpacking, backcountry camping, winter camping, cross country skiing, snowshoeing and climbing. ADK is active in trail and lean-to maintenance, conducts environmental education workshops and programs, and lobbies to encourage sound conservation. It is an active, committed group.

Adirondack Nature Conservancy and Land Trust (ANC/ALT). Established in 1971, the Adirondack Nature Conservancy is a chapter of the Nature Conservancy, an international organization. The Adirondack chapter's mission is to preserve the plants, animals and natural communities that represent the diversity of life in the Adirondacks by protecting the lands and waters they need to survive. Sound science is the foundation of ANC's work.

The Adirondacks are designated by the Nature Conservancy as one of the world's last "Great Places." ANC/ALT seeks ways to maintain a compatible economy that thrives on and protects the region's vast natural resources.

The Adirondack Land Trust (ALT). This is a local organization established in 1984 to preserve the agriculture, forest and open space lands of the greater Adirondack region's eleven million acres. Working together since 1988, the partners have been in-volved in the protection of some 225,000 acres. ANC/ALT maintains fourteen preserves totaling 7,000 acres. Most of the land protected is in private hands.

Bat Conservation International (BCI). Based in Austin, Texas, BCI is devoted to conservation, education and research initiatives involving bats and the ecosystems they serve. It was founded in 1982 as scientists around the world became concerned about the alarming decline of bats that play ecological and economic roles vital to human interests. Under the founding guidance of Merlin Tuttle, an internationally recognized authority on bats, the organization has achieved unprecedented progress by emphasizing sustainable uses of natural resources in a manner that benefits both bats and people.

In 1996 BCI worked with the Adirondack Chapter of the Nature Conservancy to evaluate and protect Graphite Mine near Albany. The mine harbors more than 100,000 little and big Brown Bats each winter, as well as the northernmost population of Indiana Bats. It is one of the most significant sites in the northeast.

The autumn sunset is nature's farewell to the end of another season, another era and another millennium. Photographed in Saratoga County.

Photographic Notes

I own three 35mm cameras with lenses from 18mm to 300mm, plus a seven-element 2X extender, a series of close-up lenses and numerous filters.

Filters give control over a vast range of factors that can make or break a photograph. They record a scene as you'd like it to appear, create a mood, flatter a subject or render an image that looks unrealistic.

For most of the photos in this book, one of these four filters was used: a polarizer, warming filter, enhancing filter or a neutral density graduating filter.

The polarizer, used on bright sunny days, reduces glare on water and foliage and increases color saturation. Its maximum effect is when the scene is at a 90° angle from the sun.

The #81B warming filter, which is a light amber color, reduces bluishness on shots taken on cloudy, overcast days or in the shade.

The enhancing filter, which is pale lavender (except under fluorescent lighting where it appears pale green), works to enhance reds and oranges without having any effect on the other colors. This is especially good to use on fall foliage or flowers.

The neutral density graduating filter is half-neutral density and half-clear. I use this on views where the background is much brighter than the foreground. The filter will subdue the bright light in the distance without under-exposing the foreground. To use this filter, the shutter and aperture must be set manually, metering the scene first without the filter.

With today's computers, photographs now can be altered and changed in countless ways.

The type of film used for the photos in this book was either Kodachrome 64, 200 or Ektachrome E100S professional film.

Mystery Picture

Park your car at the end of a dirt road, make a forty minute bushwhack with a 700' elevation gain and you'll see this impressive view. Some hunters use this area in the fall, but very few hikers. A few photos in this book have been shot around and near this hill.

Can you identify the place and view?

Stone lean-to, summit of Mount Marcy in the 1920's.